Colors in Nature

Green

Lisa Bruce

Raintree

Chicago, Illinois

Printed and bound in the United States at Lake Book Manufacturing, Inc.
07 06 05 04 03
10 9 8 7 6 5 4 3 2 1

Library of Congress Cataloging-in-Publication Data:
Bruce, Lisa.
 Green / Lisa Bruce.
    p. cm. -- (Colors in nature)
Includes index.
Summary: A simple introduction to green things found in nature.
 ISBN 1-4109-0722-8 (lib. bdg.) -- ISBN 1-4109-0727-9 (pbk.)
 1. Color in nature--Juvenile literature. 2. Green--Juvenile
literature. [1. Green. 2. Nature. 3. Color.] I. Title. II. Series:
Bruce, Lisa. Colors in nature.
 QC495.5.B765 2004
 535.6--dc22

                         2003015279

Acknowledgments
The publishers would like to thank the following for permission to reproduce photographs: pp. 4, 5 Pat & Tom
Leeson/Science Photo Library; p. 6 John Walmsley; p. 7 Robert Harding Picture Library; pp. 8, 9 Iam Beames/Ardea;
p. 10 Hermann Eisenbeiss/Science Photo Library, pp. 11l, 11b.r. Gusto/Science Photo Library; p. 11t.r. Jeremy Burgess/
Science Photo Library; pp. 12, 13 John Cancalosi/Bruce Coleman, Inc.; pp. 14, 15 Digital Vision/Getty Images; pp. 16,
17 ImageState; pp. 18, 19 Francois Gohier/Ardea; pp. 20, 21 Damien Lovegrove/Science Photo Library; p. 21r David
Solzberg/Acestock/Science Photo Library; pp. 22, 23 John Heseltine/Science Photo Library

Cover photograph by Hermann Eisenbeiss/Science Photo Library

Some words are shown in bold, **like this.** You can find out
what they mean by looking in the glossary on page 24.

Contents

Green in Nature

There are lots of green things in nature.

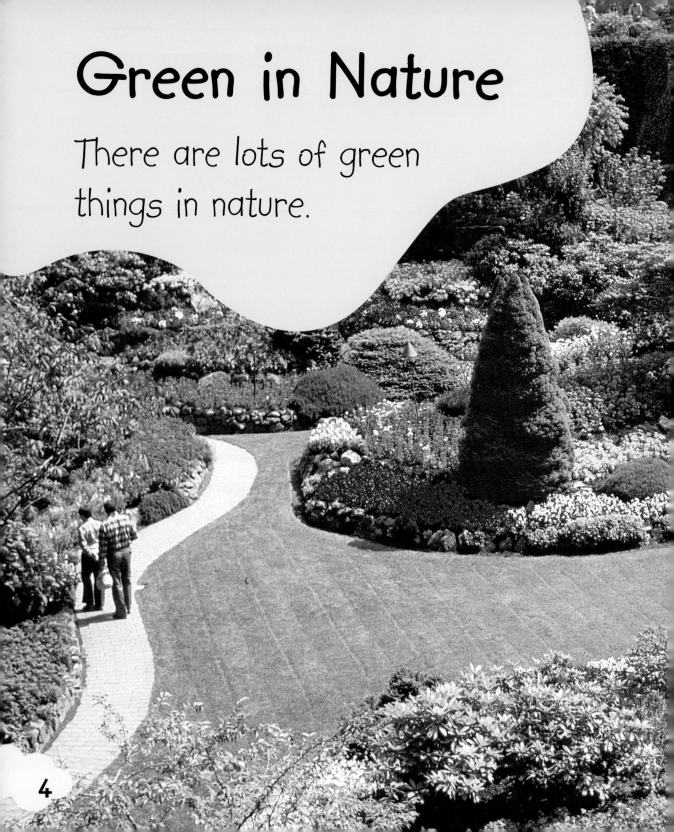

Where can you see
green in this park?

Green Leaves

The leaves on this tree are green.

Leaves come in many shapes and sizes.

Green Grass

Grass is green.

There is green grass in this soccer field.

There is green grass in this **lawn.**

Green Frogs

Some frogs are green.

They live in green ponds.

11

Green Snakes

This snake is green.

It slides softly in the green grass.

Green Birds

These green birds are called parrots.

Parrots live in jungles.

Green Bugs

Green bugs can hide on green leaves.
This green bug is a cricket.

Green Caterpillars

Some caterpillars are green.
Caterpillars eat green leaves.

Green Food

currants

broccoli

zucchini

Here are some green foods.

Can you think of more foods that are green?

brussels sprouts

grapes

cabbage

Changing Color

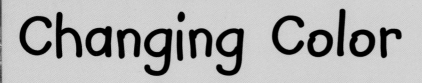

When fruits **ripen**, they change color.

New strawberries are green.

Ripe strawberries are red.
Now, you can eat them!

Glossary

currant   small green fruit that grows on a bush

jungle   forest that is in a hot, wet place

lawn   large area of grass planted outside

lily pad   large leaf of a plant that grows in water

ripen   to become ready to pick or eat

zucchini   (You say zoo-KEE-nee.) kind of squash that grows in gardens

Answer to question on page 21: There are lots of green foods! Green beans, lettuce, peas, and some apples are green.

Index